Totally Bonkers
Physics Joke Book

illy Puns, Inside Jokes & "Mass" Laughter

This book belongs to

Have you heard the new theory about inertia?

It doesn't seem to be gaining any momentum.

What is the most careful particle?

A caut-ion.

Why can't you trust an atom?

They make up everything.

What's a wavelength's favorite animal?

A lamb, duh.

What do you call a physicist who steals energy?

A joule thief.

How did the two helium atoms react after hearing a joke?

He He.

Why did the piece of wood get fired from its job on the train?

Because it was a poor conductor.

Why didn't the physicist buy the telescope to see outer space?

Because the cost was astronomical.

What type of car does a physicist drive?

A Volts-wagon.

What type of car does a rich physicist drive?

A Lambda-ghini.

Who should you call if you need to track down criminals who are good at resisting arrest?

Sherlock Ohms.

How many astronomers does it take to change a light bulb?

Two. One to change the light bulb and the other to complain about the light pollution.

How does a German physicist drink his beer?

With Ein Stein.

What does a physicist order at the seaside restaurant?

Fission chips.

What is critical mass?

A room full of movie reviewers.

Student: What's the unit for joules per second?

Teacher: Correct.

What shouldn't you ever date an atom?

Because they make up a bunch of stuff before splitting on you.

Have you heard that physicists have discovered a new particle that only exists by absorbing joy?

It's no laughing matter.

Which fish is made up of two sodium atoms?

2 Na.

How did the particle physicist escape from his laboratory without being noticed?

He created a diverse ion.

What do you call a scientist who splits atoms to create bubbly drinks?

A nuclear fizzicist.

Why does a 5 oz burger have less energy than a 5 oz steak?

Because it is in its ground state.

Why did the physicist say after finishing the wave experiment?

"Ouch, my head hertz."

Why can't you take electricity to social outings?

Because it doesn't know how to conduct itself.

Which part of the physics book is the hardest to get through?

The chapter on friction.

A photon checked into a hotel and the porter offered to help with its suitcase.

The photon replied, "I didn't bring any luggage. I'm traveling light."

A neutron walks into a bar and asks, "How much for a beer?"

The bartender smiles broadly and says, "For you, no charge."

Why did the chicken cross the road?

Isaac Newton: Chickens at rest tend to stay at rest, chickens in motion tend to cross roads.

What do you call a group of 12 atoms?

Dozen matter.

What is Einstein's DJ name?

MC Squared.

Did you hear about the belt of Joules?

It was a waste of energy.

Why didn't the sun go to college?

Because it already had a million degrees.

Did you know that Einstein took years to develop a theory about space?

And, it was about time too.

Which is faster, heat or cold?

Heat, because you can catch a cold.

What unit of energy do you get from beef?

Cowlories.

How did the duck greet the atomic physicist?

Quark, quark, quark!

A boy asks his physicist father if the moon provides light and heat to support life on Earth through nuclear fusion.

His father replies, "No sun."

How did the Professor of Electromagnetism solve the complex problem?

He used inductive reasoning.

What is relativity?

When the extended family meets together.

Why should you never ask a physicist about the relationship between electromagnetism and light?

Because he may end up talking Faraday or two.

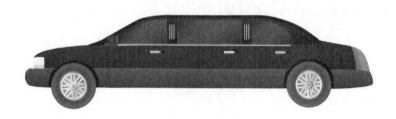

What do you call the spot where limousines are parked at the superstore?

Hyperspace.

Why did the proton have to go for therapy?

Because it is not easy being positive all the time.

Did you hear the theory about anti-friction?

It is hard to grasp.

What did the uranium-238 nucleus say at the end of the party?

Got to split!

What is 2 times 2?

Physicist: "I am fairly sure it somewhere between 3.81 and 4.13."

What is Doctor Pepper's PhD in?

Particle Fizzics.

What did the male magnet say to the female magnet?

When I saw you from the back, I thought you were repulsive. But when I saw you from the front, I found you rather attractive.

Two theoretical physicists are lost in the desert. The first theoretical physicist takes out a map and looks at it for a while.

Then he turns to the second theoretical physicist and says, "I've got it. I know where we are."

The second physicist says, "Okay, where are we?"

The first physicist replies, "Do you see that sand dune over there?"

"Yes," replied the second physicist.

"That's where we are," answered the first physicist.

An electron and a positron leave the cinema after watching a movie.

Positron: "I've lost my wallet."

Electron: "Are you sure?"

Positron: "I'm positive."

Why did Paul Dirac, Erwin Schrödinger and Wolfgang Pauli work in very small garages?

Because they were quantum mechanics.

The physicist bought a jumper from the store but he found that it kept picking up static. He took it back to the shop the next day and got a new one free of charge.

Why did the physicist call the pie in the oven an "electric pie"?

Because it was full of currants.

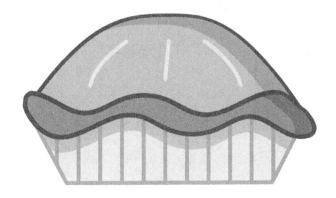

Why don't physicists wear black socks?

They're afraid of getting black holes.

What do you call a t-shirt with gravy stains on it?

Gravy Tee.

Why did Mr Ohm marry Mrs Ohm?

He couldn't resist her.

Why is it hard to be friends with an electron?

Because they are always negative.

How did the physicist feel after he lost the keys to his underground research lab?

He was very con-CERN-ed.

A physicist found his colleague, who was working on constants, lying flat on the floor.

"What are you doing?" he asked.

"Just Plancking."

Why was the physicist covered from head to toe in rope and yarn?

He was working on string theory.

Did you hear the joke about electrons losing their charge?

I could you tell but I don't want to Bohr you with it.

Why was the physics book always unhappy?

Because it was full of problems.

During a physics class, a student asked what happened before the Big Bang. However, the teacher couldn't explain, because there was no time.

Did you hear about the quarks who broke the laws of physics?

They were sent to confinement.

A physicist stands on a street corner with a bird on his shoulder. The bird starts squawking, "Pieces of seven!" repeatedly.

A passer-by stops and asks, "What's wrong with the bird?"

The physicist replies, "Broken parity."

Why do the proton and electron always make the neutron order at the restaurant?

Because there's never any charge.

Why are protons good at inspiring others?

Because they are always positive.

What do you call a subatomic particle that acts in a weird manner?

A strange quark.

How many theoretical physicists does it take to change a light bulb?

Two. One to hold the light bulb and one to rotate the universe.

Why are photons the friendliest particles?

Because they're always waving.

What happened to the beam of light that was caught speeding?

It ended up in prism.

What did the nuclear physicist say before getting into a fight with the geophysicist?

Let me atom!

Did you hear about the physicist's son who kept chewing on electrical cords?

He had to be grounded.

Did you hear about the new anti-gravity textbook?

It's impossible to put down.

What do you call space that keeps running in circles and jumping all about with too much energy?

Hyperspace.

Why were the horses in the meadow unable to move after they got horseshoes?

Because they were in a magnetic field.

What do you call one kilogram of figs falling to the ground?

1 Fig Newton.

Did you hear about the report I did on wind energy?

It was a breeze.

What did one physicist say to the other physicist after watching "Star Wars"?

May the mass times acceleration be with you!

Why did the physicist's pocket vibrate?

Because he left his phonon.

What's the fastest form of communication?

Sign language. It travels at the speed of light.

Did you hear about the man who was cooled to minus 273 degrees Celsius?

He is OK now.

Why did the physicist go on a caravan holiday?

Because he liked the convenience of travelling with a mobile ohm.

How did the electrical circuit feel after it was thrown into a pool of water?

It was shocked.

Did you hear the joke about energy being destroyed?

It doesn't matter.

Two atoms bumped into each other.

"I think I've lost an electron!" said one.

"Are you sure?" replied the other.

"I'm positive!"

Did you hear about the student who was called Kinetic by his teacher?

He had no potential.

Did you hear about the restaurant that was setup on the Moon?

Great food but no atmosphere.

Did you hear about the incident with the power socket?

"Watt?"

What type of energy does Hell run on?

Sin-ergy.

Did you hear what happened to entropy?

It isn't what it used to be.

What is the difference between entropy and atrophy?

Entropy is the measurement of the energy in a system or process that is not available to do work. Atrophy is what you get for coming in first in a race.

What's the difference between an auto mechanic and a quantum mechanic?

The quantum mechanic can get the car inside the garage without opening the door.

What is relative velocity?

The speed that you run in the opposite direction of your relatives.

What did the dog say to his owner?

My favorite frequency is 50,000 hertz but you've probably never heard of it.

What happens to physicists as they get older?

Their wavefunctions go to zero as time goes to infinity.

What did one electron say to the other electron at the party?

Don't get excited or you will get into a state!

What do physicists enjoy doing the most at sporting events?

Doing the wave.

Why don't neutrons ever end up in jail?

Because they're never charged.

Child 1: Did you know that sound cannot travel in a vacuum?

Child 2: That's not true. My vacuum at home is super noisy.

Is studying radioactivity hard?

No, it is as easy as alpha, beta and gamma.

In which town do people move the fastest?

Velo City.

Einstein, Newton and Pascal were playing Hide and Seek. Einstein slowly counted to 100 while Pascal ran off and hid.

Newton drew a one meter by one meter square on the floor and sat down in the center of the square.

When Einstein finished counting, he opened his eyes and spotted Newton. "That was easy, I found you Newton!"

Newton replied, "No you didn't, I'm Pascal."

When the boy refused to run anymore, his mother asked him why.

He replied, "Because I heard that the faster you go, the shorter you become."

What was Schrödinger's favorite childhood book?

The Cat in the Box by Dr. Seuss

Why did the chicken cross the Mobius strip?

Because it wanted to get to the same side.

A block of dry ice began to turn into carbon dioxide gas.

After it had turned into a cloud of carbon dioxide, an oxygen cloud nearby asks, "Hey, I just saw you go through a phase change...how was it?"

The carbon dioxide cloud replied, "It was sublime."

After a fight, the girlfriend told her physicist boyfriend that she needed time and distance.

As she walked away, he was left confused about why she needed to calculate velocity.

A scientist drops a piano and a flashlight from a 20-storey building.

He observes that they both hit the ground at the same time. What does he conclude from this experiment?

Pianos move at the speed of light.

A helium atom walked into the bar. The bartender says, "We don't serve noble gases here".

It didn't react.

Where is the speed of sound faster than the speed of light?

At the traffic lights, when the car behind starts to horn before the lights even turn green.

Why did a scientist install a door knocker?

Because he wanted to a no-bell prize.

What did the thermometer say to the graduated cylinder?

You may have graduated but I've got many degrees.

A boy was running around very fast while doing his homework late at night.

His mother asked him why he was running while holding a book.

He replied, "I heard that time slows down the faster you go and I need more time to finish my homework."

What sign did the nuclear physicist hang on his laboratory door when he was on holiday?

Gone Fission.

Two cats are sliding down a roof. Which one falls off first?

The one with the smaller "mew" (μ or mu).

Why did the physicist eat photons after lunch?

He needed a light snack.

Did you hear about the upcoming seminar on time travel?

It was held two weeks ago.

H_2O is the formula for water. What is the formula for ice?

H_2O cubed.

Did you hear about the nuclear physicist who had more projects than he could handle?

He had too many ions in the fire.

Why is that even though photons from a rainbow hit you at 300 million m/s, you don't feel it?

Because they are pretty light.

What did one photon say to the other photon?

I'm sick and tired of your interference.

Have you seen the documentary about WD-40?

It is non-friction.

Did you hear the story about air resistance?

It's such a drag.

Teacher: Does anyone have any questions ahead of tomorrow's exam?

Student: Can you go over terminal velocity?

Teacher: No.

Why do you have to be careful when calculating frequency?

Because it Hertz.

What do you call a group of atoms are super emotional?

Mass hysteria.

Did you hear that Iron Man and the Silver Surfer are teaming up?

They are now alloys.

The optimist sees the glass half full. The pessimist sees the glass half empty. The physicist sees the glass completely full, half with liquid and half with gas.

Why are superconductors are always being taken advantage of?

Because they never offer any resistance.

What did the physics student call the mean kid in school?

The derivative of acceleration.

Why do people hate gravity?

Because it holds them down.

Why should you be wary of any diet that recommends light eating?

Because you may become a black hole.

What led the physics teacher to break up with the biology Teacher?

There was no chemistry.

What do pirates and photons have in common?

They both travel at c.

What do you call a reboot of the classic sci-fi film TRON?

Neu-tron.

What measure of time has the least weight?

A Light Year.

How do you organize a party in space?

You planet.

Why did the kid give up on his dream to be an astronaut?

Because his parents said "The Sky's the Limit".

What does a Greek cow say?

Mu.

Do you know why energy isn't made up of atoms?

It doesn't matter.

How heavy is a truck made of light?

Photons.

How do you make sure you don't lose an electron?

Keep an ion it.

Why did the physicist buy a book about photons?

He needed some light reading.

An ultra low frequency sine wave walks into a bar.

The bartender says, "Why the long phase?"

Albert Einstein created new physics concepts.

His brother, Frank, however, created a monster.

Gravity is one of the most important forces in the universe.

Without "it", you just end up with gravy.

What do you call a 1 trillion pins?

A terrapin.

What footwear has the least friction?

Slippers.

Why is the moon more useful than the sun?

Because the moon shines at night when you need light. The sun shines during the day when you don't need it.

How many physicists does it take to change a light bulb?

Ten. One to do it and nine to co-author the paper.

How many radio astronomers does it take to change a light bulb?

None. They are not interested in short wave stuff.

A cop pulled over a Spanish photon for speeding.

The cop asked, "Do you know how fast you were going?"

The photon replied, "c."

A physics professor retires and buys a lake house.

He builds two long wooden platforms out over the lake and every day he takes a bow and shoots arrows into the lake.

One day, a curious neighbor asks him what he is doing.

The physicist replies, "I've always been interested in the archer's pair of docks."

Want to hear a joke about neutrinos?

It will probably go straight through you.

Why did the scientist name his son Physics?

He wanted to be known as the Father of Physics.

Why do mother's like Newton's second law?

Because it proves that "MA" is a force to be reckoned with.

Why did the physics professor make his class sit at the edge of a cliff?

Because that's where they had the most potential.

Why was the ice cube feeling grumpy as it turned into water?

It was going through a phase.

Why are protons, neutrons and electrons important?

Because the little things matter.

A Flat Earther snuck into a physics seminar and while the speaker was talking about gravity, he shouted, "What makes you think that gravity is real?"

The speaker dropped the mic.

One day, a physics teacher said to the class: "Let's do some revision. What is Fouriers Law?" A students raises his hand and answers correctly.

Teacher: "Good. Now, what is Lamberts Cosine Law?" Another student raises her hand and answers correctly.

Teacher: "Excellent. Let's try one more. Cole's Law?" This time, no hands went up.

Teacher: "I'm sure you know this, class. Cole's Law?" Still no response.

Teacher: "I'm surprised you don't know this. Cole's Law is a shredded raw cabbage mixed with mayonnaise!"

Why did the chicken cross the road?

Albert Einstein: Whether the chicken crossed the road or the road crossed under the chicken depends on your frame of reference.

Why did the chicken cross the road?

Werner Heisenberg: It cannot be determined exactly which side of the road the chicken was on, but it was moving very fast.

Why did the physicist only invite 3 VIPs to his party?

Because he only wanted 3 significant figures.

What happens when you cross a mosquito with a snake?

Nothing. You can't cross a vector and a scalar.

Why are physicists always relaxed?

Because they know how to solve tension-related problems.

A policeman came across a child crying on the street corner. Concerned, the policeman asked the boy, "What's the matter?"

The boy looked at the policeman and said, "A substance that has mass and occupies space."

X asked X^2: "Do you believe we are alone in the universe?"

X^2 replied, "No, I believe in higher powers."

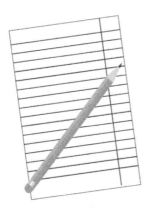

Did you hear about the student who mixed up temperature units while doing his physics test?

He got an absolute zero.

Did you hear about the scientist who was obsessed with the difference between cosine and sine?

Turns out that it was just a phase.

What did the positive charge say to the negative charge after their first date?

We have potential.

What type of particles does IKEA emit?

Futons.

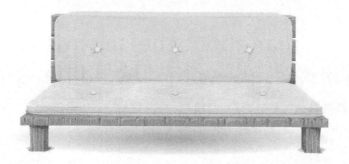

What is an electron?

What the US did in 1980 and 1984 when they chose Ronald Reagan as president.

What do you call a dinosaur that falls off the top of the Empire State Building?

Terminal velociraptor.

Did you hear the joke about thermodynamics?

It still hasn't reached equilibrium yet.

A son asks his physicist father, "Daddy, what is string theory?"

The father replies, "Why are you asking me such difficult questions? Ask me something easier."

The son then asks, "Um, ok. Why does mommy get so angry sometimes?"

"String theory is a theoretical framework of everything where point-like particles..."

Did you hear the joke about muons?

I would repeat it but I'd be breaking some laws.

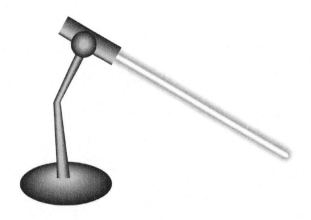

Did you hear about the new equipment that is being developed to capture protons?

So far, the results have been positive.

What do you call someone who destroys a group of Higgs Boson particles?

A mass murderer.

What equipment can you use to watch particles accelerating and colliding in pretty patterns?

A collider-scope.

How many physicists does it take to screw in a lightbulb?

Approximating the lightbulb as a point particle, assuming it takes place in a vacuum, assuming it takes place at precisely 200 K and ignoring the Heisenberg Uncertainty Principle, $\pi^2/5$.

A physicist and another man are travelling through the desert in a car. After a while, the physicist realizes that he is lost. He turns to the other man and asks, "Do you know where are we?"

The man replies, "We are in a car."

The physicist pauses for a moment and asks the other man, "You are a mathematician, right?"

"Yes, how did you know?"

"Easy, your answer was 100% correct and 100% useless."

Who do you call to fix an atom?

Call a quantum mechanic.

What did the molecule say to the atom after he got in trouble?

I've got my ion you.

What did the neutron say to the proton in the nucleus?

Thanks for letting me live here free of charge!

Did you hear about the two atomic bombs that got into an argument?

They had a fallout.

Why is losing weight is like an atom losing electrons?

Because everything is positive after that.

Two scientists see atoms for the first time.

Scientist 1: So everything is made up of these tiny particles?

Scientist 2: I guess so.

Scientist 1: What should we call these things?

Scientist 2: Do we have to name it? Is it important?

Scientist 1: Yes, I think it Matters.

What speed do the particles in the Large Hadron Collider travel at?

Super cern-ic.

What's the most terrifying word in nuclear physics?

"Oops!"

Why are photons the saddest particles?

They keep hearing people say that they don't matter.

Did you hear the bad joke about frequencies?

It hertz.